D1509649

Murderer

MURDERER

a play in two acts

Anthony Shaffer

MARION BOYARS

LONDON · BOSTON

Published simultaneously in Great Britain
and the United States in 1979
By Marion Boyars Publishers Ltd.
18 Brewer Street, London W1R 4AS.
        and
Marion Boyars Publishers Inc.
99 Main St, Salem, New Hampshire 03079

Australian distribution by Thomas C. Lothian
4-12 Tattersalls Lane, Melbourne, Victoria 3000.

Canadian distribution by Burns & MacEachern Ltd.
Suite 3, 62 Railside Road, Don Mills, Ontario.

        ISBN 0 7145 2544 8 cased   edition
             0 7145 2545 6 paperback edition

Printed and bound in Great Britain by
Redwood Burn Ltd, Trowbridge and Esher

Cast

Norman Bartholomew
Sergeant Stenning
Millie Sykes
Elizabeth Bartholomew

Act One

Scene One

Thirty minutes should elapse between the start of the play and the first spoken words "Open up. Police."

The artist's studio cum living room of NORMAN
BARTHOLOMEW, *in a small village in Dorset, England.
The usual painter's paraphernalia litters the place, and
many canvases lie against the walls. Upstage left is the
kitchen area containing* inter alia, *a gas stove. Next to the
stove, is a sink. Upstage right of kitchen is a passage leading
off to an unseen hallway. Centre stage is the living area
containing a sofa, sofa table with lamp and a large pot-
bellied stove, vigorously alight. Centre stage is a divan.
Above this is a staircase leading to a bathroom and offstage
bedroom. The double frosted glass doors leading into the
bathroom are closed. (NB. An alternative and effective way
of showing the bathroom is to have walls of gauze, so that
when it is in use it can be lit and visible to the whole
auditorium, and when not in use it would be opaque).
Downstage right is a desk and desk chair. Positioned with its
back to us in front of the stove is an armchair and foot
stool. The time is about five o'clock on a winter's evening.
A winter sunset highlights statues and withered pot plants,
in an outside garden room. As the curtain rises* NORMAN
BARTHOLOMEW, *a good-looking smooth man dressed
casually in slacks and jumper is standing at an easel painting,
standing behind him, watching him paint is an attractive girl
in her early twenties. Threatening music can either come
from a radio or perhaps better, be overlaid at appropriate
moments throughout the scene to highlight the tension. She
leaves him and gets a magazine from the sofa, and sits in the
armchair facing up towards* NORMAN. *He stops painting
and goes to pour two drinks, the bottle is empty, he gets
another one from the cellar, pours the drinks and goes to
the kitchen to put water in them. He gives the girl her
drink, and returns to his easel. He regards her slyly from
time to time as she starts to sip her drink. Finally she drains
it, and after a pause there is a crash as the glass slips from
her fingers and she slumps unconscious. He crosses rapidly
to the chair, and takes a scarf from the back of it. This he*

9

puts carefully round the girl's throat and pulls it tight. With much grunting and straining he maintains the pressure for a full minute.

BARTHOLOMEW *examines her critically, taking her pulse, listening to her heart etc. satisfied that she is dead, he delicately picks out the scarf from the folds of the neck, burns it in the stove. He then takes the body from the chair, and carries it to the sofa stage right, where he lays it carefully face down. Suddenly he stiffens, as if hearing a noise, and stands still listening. He goes quietly through to the front door and opens it. After a long moment, he closes it and locks it and returns to the body.*

One by one he removes the shoes, stockings, skirt, blouse and underclothes, and takes them into the bedroom.

He returns with a blanket in which he wraps the corpse.

His next action is to take a pair of pliers and remove a number of teeth from the head. These he puts in a glass dish and pours acid on them from a glass-stoppered bottle. Fumes rise from the dish.

Now he picks up the blanket-wrapped corpse and carries it up the stairs to the bathroom. We see him tip it out into the bath, with a dull, soft thud. He then folds the blanket neatly and descends the stairs with it closing the door behind him and disappears into the bedroom.

A few moments pass and he re-appears stripped off down to his shorts, in which state he crosses the stage into the dining area where he puts on a full chef's apron. He also selects a butcher's knife and a meat saw, and places them on a central table.

He then descends to the cellar and returns with half a dozen sacks which he places next to them. A car light passes the

10

*window and we hear the car slow and stop. In a sudden
panic he rushes to the window and looks out. After a long
moment the car starts and the lights move on. With a sigh of
relief he leaves the window and moves back to the kitchen
where he gives himself a large whisky, and smokes a calming
cigarette. He examines his hand which is shaking. Gradually
it stops.*

*Now he takes the knife, saw and sack upstairs to the bath-
room, and gets to work on the body in the bath. He begins
with the knife and then changes to the saw, and we hear the
very explicit noise of it cutting through bone. Eventually
we see him straighten up holding an arm which he puts in a
sack. He then starts on the other arm using first the knife,
and then the saw. Eventually he succeeds in detaching it
and, holding up the hand, he takes off the ring from the
ring finger. He then puts the arm in another sack.*

*Carrying the two sacks he leaves the bathroom and crosses
to the stove. He throws them in, where they start to sizzle
furiously. Suddenly we see his apron is covered in blood, as
are his hands. He now lights a blow torch and melts the ring
in a pestle. He throws the mess in the stove.*

*Suddenly a newspaper is pushed abruptly through the letter
box and slaps on the floor. He jumps and stoops to pick it
up. The headline reads 'Torso Found In Tea Chest'. The
photograph is of the accused with a coat over his head being
escorted by Police Officers. He sits down to read it with
evident pleasure. After a moment or two he rises and
throws down the paper, now bloodstained.*

*He now returns to the bathroom taking up to it an electric
drill with garden saw attachment and goes to work on a leg.
The task is extremely strenuous, but he finally succeeds in
detaching it with much cracking and whirring from the
electric saw and puts it in a sack. He crosses again to the
furnace and throws it in.*

11

*A timer clock rings startling him. Wiping his sweating brow
with the back of his forearm, he crosses to the kitchen and
puts on the kettle. He then opens the oven and takes out a
spit on which is a roast of beef. He detaches the meat and
puts in on a plate. The spit and prongs he washes, dries and
replaces in the oven. He regards the roast of rare beef
fondly, comparing its colour and texture with his own
dripping hands. Fastidiously he washes them under a tap
before carving off a decent slice and making himself a neat
sandwich which he seasons elaborately with salt, pepper and
mustard. Primly he cuts off all the crusts. He starts to eat it
as he saunters back to the bathroom to start work on the
last limb.*

*Before picking up the knife, he carefully props the plate
with the sandwich on the side of the bath, takes a bite, and
munches cheerfully as he cuts. Putting down the knife, he
starts sawing, but the vibrations succeed in tipping his
sandwich and plate into the bath. He retrieves the plate and
then the sandwich, which he is about to take a bite out of,
when he sees it saturated with blood. Briefly he debates
eating it, but reluctantly rejects the idea, replaces it on the
plate, and puts it on the floor. He continues with the sawing
until he achieves a successful severance, whereupon he puts
the leg in a sack and once again walks down the stairs to the
stove.*

*Halfway across the room there is a sudden piercing shriek.
Involuntarily he drops the sack, and whirls round to face
the bathroom, as if fearing the corpse had come alive.
Almost immediately he realises it is only the kettle and
grins ruefully to himself. He picks up the sack with the leg
in it and tosses it into the stove before crossing to the kettle
and turning it off. He makes himself a cup of instant coffee,
and lights a cigarette which he inhales deeply.*

*Now he picks up a chopper from the wood basket and
returns to the bathroom where he sets to work to cut off*

the head. The blows are deliberate and sickening. After
three or four he straightens up, holding the head by its hair.
He examines it closely, then kisses it playfully on the nose.

Suddenly the telephone shrills. He drops the head back in
the bath and takes some involuntary running steps down
the stairs towards the instrument. Then he pauses, listening
to it ring, goes to it and is about to lift the receiver when he
stops himself. In an agony of indecision he stands with his
bloody hand held out above the telephone. Finally it stops
and he retraces his steps to the bathroom where he packs
both the torso and the head in sacks and carries them over
to the stove and throws them in.

Returning to the bathroom he scrubs the floor round the
bath, then cleans the electric saw, handsaw, knife and
hatchet in the bath, and walks downstairs to replace them
in their original places — the chopper in the wood basket,
and the saws and knife in the kitchen.

Now he goes back to the bathroom to scrub out the bath
meticulously, and then strips himself for an intensive wash.
He dries himself and then walks down into the bedroom to
dress, hanging the blood-stained apron over the banisters, as
he goes. In the bedroom we hear him whistling cheerfully as
he dresses.

Suddenly the doorbell sounds. The whistling stops abruptly.
He emerges from the bedroom wearing sweater and slacks,
and looks anxiously towards the front door and then at the
stove. He stands indecisively doing nothing. It sounds again,
impatiently. Slowly he goes towards the front door, and is
about to open it when he checks himself and looks round to
examine the room for any signs of his recent activity. As
the door bell sounds again he sees the bloodstained apron
hanging over the banisters.

SERGEANT
STENNING
> *(off)* Open up! Police!

> *He runs quickly across stage and up the stairs to retrieve the apron, and then down again to thrust it into the stove. He then runs to the front door and throws it open.*

BARTHOLOMEW.
> *(off)* Sorry to keep you. I was in the bath.

STENNING.
> *(off)* Is that so sir? In the bath eh? Would you mind if I stepped inside?

BARTHOLOMEW.
> *(off)* Why should I?

STENNING.
> *(off)* I think it would be better, sir?

BARTHOLOMEW.
> *(off)* I mean mind. Come in.

STENNING.
> *(off)* Thank you, sir.

> *STENNING enters, removing his cap as he does so and putting it down. He is somewhat younger than BARTHOLOMEW and a good deal heavier.*

> It is Mr. Bartholomew, isn't it? Mr. Norman Bartholomew?

BARTHOLOMEW.
> Mr. Norman Cresswell Bartholomew actually. And you're Sergeant Stenning aren't you? How can I help you.

> *STENNING looks slowly round the room. He is obviously*

uncomfortable.

STENNING.
It's a little difficult to explain, sir, and I trust you won't take offence, but well you see we've got to investigate all complaints even if they are ... .

BARTHOLOMEW.
Yes?

STENNING.
Well, fanciful like.

BARTHOLOMEW.
Fanciful like?

STENNING.
Well, barmy, sir. You know — a bit out to lunch.

BARTHOLOMEW.
I can quite see that Sergeant, but I do hope nobody has been making fanciful, barmy, or out to lunch statements about me.

STENNING.
I'm afraid as a matter of fact they have, sir.

BARTHOLOMEW.
I'm sorry to hear that. Nothing serious I trust.

STENNING.
Very serious, I'm sorry to say. Very serious indeed.

BARTHOLOMEW.
I know. I've been pissing on Mrs. Green's sunflowers again?

STENNING.
I did say it was extremely serious.

BARTHOLOMEW.
The vicar's found the fly buttons I put in the plate last Sunday?

STENNING *stares at* BARTHOLOMEW *blank-eyed.*
BARTHOLOMEW *continues somewhat discomforted.*

BARTHOLOMEW.
Perhaps he's put them on that old grey suit of his. They've been missing for the last couple of years. As a matter of fact it's him you ought to be interrogating. I'm absolutely convinced he spends his afternoons on the common disguised as a tramp, flashing the secondary-school girls.

STENNING.
I haven't come about the vicar, sir.

BARTHOLOMEW.
Well what the devil have you come about?

STENNING.
Mrs. Ramage, who as you know, has the cottage behind you, called the station a few minutes ago, and said she saw you through that big window there, acting in a highly suspicious manner.

BARTHOLOMEW *looks uneasily at the window, as if he'd forgotten it.*

BARTHOLOMEW.
Suspicious manner?

STENNING.
Criminal would be nearer the mark.

BARTHOLOMEW.
Bomb making, or buggery?

STENNING.
> Strangling a woman.

BARTHOLOMEW.
> A woman . . . But I've been all alone here this evening . . .

STENNING.
> She couldn't be sure, but she thought it might be your wife.
> After which, she said she saw you take the clothes off the
> body, and then get undressed yourself.

BARTHOLOMEW.
> My God, who'd have thought old Mrs. Ramage was a
> peeping Tom?

STENNING.
> She further said she saw you carry the body into another
> room, and return to get a saw and later a hatchet, for the
> purpose, she presumes, of dismembering it.

BARTHOLOMEW.
> *(singing)* I'll dismember you in all the old familiar places.

STENNING.
> Would you mind *not* singing, sir.

BARTHOLOMEW.
> Why not? Both Wood and Billings were recorded as having
> sung mightily after they were apprehended for hewing up
> John Hayes.

STENNING.
> What are you talking about?

BARTHOLOMEW.
> The pawnbroker, John Hayes. Killed with a coal hatchet
> under the Brawn's Head Inn, New Bond Street at the
> instigation of his wife.

STENNING.
>I've never heard of the case.

BARTHOLOMEW.
>It was all a bit before your time I expect — 1725. His wife Catherine boiled the flesh off the decapitated head to make it unrecognizable, and Messrs Wood and Billings carried it in a bucket to the Thames near Lambeth Bridge where they threw it in. It was all to no avail, however. The head was recognized and they were caught. Which only goes to show, Sergeant, that if you want to get away with spouse-disposal, you've simply got to make the body unrecognizable.

STENNING.
>*(stolidly)* Exactly so, sir. Mrs. Ramage also said she saw you carrying a number of sacks.

BARTHOLOMEW.
>You know the strangest thing is that anyone should actually recognize a pawnbroker. I mean you know — you shuffle in rather embarrassed, not looking him in the face, and muttering " 'ow much'll yer give me for this lot, guvner. It's been in the family 150 years. It's me great grandmother's twenty-four carat, solid gold dilldoll . . . must be worth a packet." . . . You know the sort of thing. But you certainly don't go in for much eyeball contact do you now?

STENNING.
>Sir! Would you please give me your attention.

BARTHOLOMEW.
>I assure you, you have it. You were telling me an improbable tale of me quartering my wife and gift-wrapping her in sacking. What exactly was I meant to have done with these parcels?

STENNING.
>She didn't know. Apparently you passed out of her line of

18

vision.

BARTHOLOMEW.
How strange. I always thought Mrs. Ramage had X-ray eyes.

STENNING.
I'd rather like to take a look round, if you don't mind. Let's
see if we can't find a boiled head or two.

BARTHOLOMEW.
Now look here Sergeant, you really can't believe all this
rubbish. I mean, do I look the sort of bloke who'd carve up
his missus?

STENNING.
In my opinion there's no one who couldn't answer to that
description.

BARTHOLOMEW.
In full sight of the neighbours?

STENNING.
As I said before, it all does sound a bit far-fetched, but I
have to check. I'm sure you understand.

BARTHOLOMEW.
I'm not sure that I do. As you can see this room is devoted
to the gentle pursuit of the Arts, Sergeant.

STENNING.
Some people believe that murder is an art, sir. Excuse me.

STENNING *walks over to the kitchen area and starts to
examine the saw and the knives which are arrayed on a
magnetised steel bar on the wall.* BARTHOLOMEW
*suddenly sees the bloodstained evening newspaper. He picks
it up, folds it inside out, and nonchalantly starts to read it.*
STENNING *shoots him a suspicious look then glances at*

the portrait of MRS. BARTHOLOMEW *on the wall.*

By the way, where exactly is your wife?

BARTHOLOMEW.
  She's away.

STENNING.
  Away? . . . Where?

BARTHOLOMEW.
  I don't know exactly. Some hospital outside Birmingham
  I think she said.

STENNING.
  You mean she's ill?

BARTHOLOMEW.
  I mean she's a gynaecological surgeon. She's doing some
  operations there.

STENNING.
  But you are expecting her back fairly shortly?

BARTHOLOMEW.
  Frankly I'm not sure that I'm expecting her back, at all.

  STENNING *shoots* BARTHOLOMEW *a curious glance.*

STENNING.
  Oh?

BARTHOLOMEW.
  Well I suppose it's no secret in the village that my wife and
  I don't particularly get on. Recently she's been hinting that
  she's found another feller, and is thinking of leaving me.

STENNING.
  I see. And may I ask what your attitude was to what she

told you.

BARTHOLOMEW.
(simulated passion) Blind brute jealousy. I'd rather cut her
up in the bath, than let another man possess her.

STENNING *regards him levelly. Suddenly* BARTHOLOMEW
bursts out laughing.

STENNING.
(affronted) Which way *is* the bathroom?

BARTHOLOMEW.
Up there.

STENNING *brushes past* BARTHOLOMEW *and makes his
way across the room and up the stairs to the bathroom.*
BARTHOLOMEW *watches his progress with some
trepidation, crossing to the bottom of the stairs for a closer
view as* STENNING *kneels to examine the bath with
minute care. After a long moment he straightens up,
apparently satisfied.*

BARTHOLOMEW.
No grimy ring, Sergeant? Would even my mother-in-law
approve as they say in those craven commercials?

STENNING.
Of your bath, sir, yes. But not, I think, of your eating
habits. I found this under it.

He produces the bloodsodden sandwich. BARTHOLOMEW
stares at it, then slowly walks up the stairs, as if mesmerized.
BARTHOLOMEW *and* STENNING *look at each other in
silence, then the former bends to peer at the sandwich.*

BARTHOLOMEW.
I'm afraid I like my roast beef rare, Sergeant. A crime I

know, in most English restaurants, but surely not in common law.

STENNING *sniffs the sandwich gingerly, and then opens it.*

STENNING.
It really is very bloody, sir. Quite sodden with it in fact.

BARTHOLOMEW.
I shouldn't waste time in idle speculation if I were you, Sergeant. Thanks to the invention of the spectroscope it has been possible to distinguish between animal and human blood for the past 84 years.

BARTHOLOMEW *takes the sandwich from the plate and takes a bite. He gags on it.* STENNING *grasps his wrist like lightning, and retrieves the remains of the sandwich, which he then places in a small cellophane bag, and pockets it.*

BARTHOLOMEW.
If you want a snack, Sergeant, you only have to ask. Didn't your mummy ever tell you it's very rude to grab.

BARTHOLOMEW *stalks down the stairs.* STENNING *follows him down, and starts prowling round the room looking in chests and cupboards for signs of the body. Near the stove he suddenly stops and sniffs. His face wrinkles in disgust and he takes a hard look at the stove which he transfers to* BARTHOLOMEW, *who flinches away from it. Briskly he steps forward, preparatory to throwing open the door.*

(involuntary) No!

STENNING *opens the door of the stove and peers inside. He recoils almost instantly.*

STENNING.
My God!

STENNING *reaches in and tries to extract something with his naked hands, but it is too hot. He looks round desperately for some implement, and he grabs a pair of fire tongs standing up against the wall. With these he drags out the head, and lets it fall on the floor, where it rolls about smoking horribly. He manages to beat out the sparks in the hair which are causing the smoke, and then drags out a partially burnt leg.* BARTHOLOMEW *watches him horror-struck backed up against a wall, apparently incapable of speech. But suddenly he starts babbling wildly.*

BARTHOLOMEW.
I had to do it, Sergeant. Can't you see that . . . She was always on at me, nagging . . . never leaving me alone . . . insanely jealous of everybody I might happen to speak to . . . Night after night, never any sleep . . . who was I with? . . . who was my lover? . . . creating scenes in public . . . hounding me wherever I went . . . making me a laughing stock . . . You do see, don't you. I had no choice.

BARTHOLOMEW *falls on to his knees sobbing.*
STENNING *who has been examining the head and leg, regards him curiously, then turns back to the task of removing parts of the body from the furnace. Eventually he picks up the head by the hair and holds it aloft. Very deliberately he taks a palette knife from a side table and knocks the skull with it. It gives off a dull, hollow sound. Alternatively he can pop out a glass eye so that it rolls across the floor.*

STENNING.
Is this some sort of sick joke? This isn't a body. It's some kind of dummy or waxwork.

BARTHOLOMEW.
To be exact it's wood. But the limbs are made of expanded polystyrene stiffened with wire and filled with stage blood — what film stuntmen refer to as Kensington Gore — made

it myself as a matter of fact.

STENNING *puts the head down on a table and turns very deliberately to face* BARTHOLOMEW.

STENNING.
(*coldly*) I think you owe me an explanation, sir?

BARTHOLOMEW.
No, I don't think I *owe* you anything, Sergeant. But because I'm a genial, gregarious sort of fellow, I'll supply you with one. Why not take a seat and make yourself comfortable.

STENNING.
No, I don't believe I will. You've been making a right pillock out of me.

BARTHOLOMEW.
Not at all. I may have been making a right pillock out of myself, but that's surely up to me.

STENNING.
And what's more, you've been obstructing me in the performance of my duties. All that stuff about murdering your wife because she was jealous.

BARTHOLOMEW.
A little play-acting that's all. The end of the fantasy has surely got to be self-justification.

STENNING.
Now you look here Mr. Bartholomew. You'd better start making some sense, or I'll take you down to the station and have the Inspector sort it out.

BARTHOLOMEW.
(*resignedly*) Oh alright!

STENNING.
To begin with — what's this here fantasy you're talking about?

BARTHOLOMEW.
Why, that I was Bukhtyar Rustomji Ratanji Hakim, of course.

STENNING.
Eh?

BARTHOLOMEW.
Better known as Buck Ruxton the Parsee doctor who in 1935 murdered his mistress and spent a whole night carefully cutting her up in a bath, draining her of blood, and making her up into neat little bundles for disposal.

STENNING.
(incredulous) You mean you've been play-acting you were him?

BARTHOLOMEW.
Exactly.

STENNING.
What in the world for?

BARTHOLOMEW.
It's very simple. I wanted to know what it felt like actually doing it — you know — the fear of a sudden caller, of tell-tale blood on clothes, of identification through teeth or jewellery.

STENNING *shakes his head in bewilderment.*

STENNING.
But you weren't actually doing it. You were just pretending. That's hardly the same thing.

BARTHOLOMEW.

    I have a very vivid imagination, Sergeant. What I may lose
in moribund verisimilitude, I gain in inventive artistry.

STENNING.

    Here, now hang on a minute. Just let me get all this straight.
You actually made this dummy and filled it with — with
stage blood, and then hacked it up in the bath simply in
order to reproduce the crime of this Doctor Buxton?

BARTHOLOMEW.

    Ruxton. Yes, I've already said so.

STENNING.

    But in God's name why?

BARTHOLOMEW.

    It gives me a thrill that's why. Oh don't look so disapproving
Sergeant. It takes all kinds, you know. Some people can't
live without the excitements of hang gliding or drag racing.
Me, I like to play famous murderers. So far I've been
Frederick Henry Seddon, the Tollington Park killer who
disposed of his tenant with arsenic, and George Chapman
who poisoned three of his so-called wives with strychnine,
and Henry Wainwright the Whitechapel Road murderer.

STENNING.

    What did he do?

BARTHOLOMEW.

    Silly man, he made the most fearsome mistake, using
chloride of lime instead of quicklime. You see it had the
effect of preserving the body of his mistress whom he had
concealed under some floorboards, rather than destroying
it.

STENNING.

    And you reconstructed that?

BARTHOLOMEW.

Indeed I did. But that wasn't the best bit. That came, when like him I took a cab across London with the disinterred remains wrapped in brown paper, in the company of an unsuspecting ballet dancer, smoking a cigar to disguise the smell. Well in my case I actually used five pounds of ancient bloaters to simulate the odour of human putrefaction, and the ballet dancer was really more of your Soho stripper, but the effect was much the same.

STENNING *looks at him aghast.*

STENNING.

You actually did that?

BARTHOLOMEW.

Certainly I did. I took the exact route he did. Down Whitechapel Street, over London Bridge to the Borough High Street, though I'm afraid the actual Ironmonger's shop were Wainwright was arrested has been demolished. It's such a shame when these old land-marks get torn down, don't you think Sergeant? Perhaps I'll found a society for the Preservation of Murder's Monuments.

STENNING *shakes his head dumbly.* BARTHOLOMEW *chuckles delightedly as he moves to pour himself a large glass of whisky.*

Will you join me?

STENNING.

Not just now. Listen, are you a bloody nutter or something?

BARTHOLOMEW.

A nutter? I don't think so. I just like to pay homage to the great murderers of the past . . . to Doctor Neil Cream who prowled Lambeth in the nineties, cross-eyed and top-hatted, dispatching ladies of the evening with *nux vomica* . . . to

27

Louis Voisin, the Charlotte Street butcher who minced his paramour into trays of offal . . . to Florence Maybrick, who, it was said, turned her husband's stomach into a druggist's drainpipe . . . Why, the very names should bring tears of grateful nostalgia to your eyes.

STENNING.
They sound like a right load of villains to me.

BARTHOLOMEW.
On the contrary they were heroes, every one — master practitioners in the world of bizarre homicide. Take the case of Patrick Mahon for example. He's particularly apropos. Surely you remember the Crumbles Bungalow murder case?

STENNING.
I can't say I can, no.

BARTHOLOMEW.
How strange. I do think that a young man with his way to make in the police force should take more interest in these things. He was a classic dismemberer. Sliced up his lady-love, Emily Kaye, in 1924 and dropped pieces of her from the train between Waterloo and Richmond Stations. I think I might have a go at him next week, though I don't suppose the exercise will do a lot for keeping Britain tidy.

STENNING.
I'm afraid I just don't understand you sir. I don't understand you at all.

BARTHOLOMEW.
That's because you don't understand the true nature of murder — that once a man has killed deliberately his inhibitions are destroyed, because he has truly looked on mortality. "He has joined the alien clan, of which no member knows the other, and has set his face against the world. Thereafter he is alone magnificent in his belief in the

impossibility of divine forgiveness."

STENNING.

That's as may be, but for me murder is a shocking crime — the most shocking, and I certainly can't see any fun in it.

BARTHOLOMEW.

It's not a question of fun exactly, but how it enables you to look at life. Can't you see that life is beautiful, and that murder is the most extreme form of the denial of man's potential to see that beauty. As such its study is of compelling interest to a curious chap like me.

STENNING.

Is it? Well, while you've been studying it, I have had to deal with it — as it is in the flesh. At various times, and in various places, I have seen the agony of murdered people, and I've smelt the odour of murdered people, and I've touched the skin of murdered people, and I can tell you there's nothing compelling about it in any way.

BARTHOLOMEW.

Yes, but can't you see that . . .

STENNING.

Do not continue to play with death, Mr. Bartholomew. I know beyond a shadow of doubt that most murder victims spend all their lives searching for their murderers. Be warned. You do not know the game you play at all well. Stop in time.

An uneasy silence.

I'll go over to Mrs. Ramage's now, and set her mind at rest. She was highly disturbed.

BARTHOLOMEW.

Mrs. Ramage is a tiresome old fart who richly deserves the

attentions of Jack the Ripper. Just imagine finding a piece of her pancreas wrapped up in a cardboard box, waiting for you when you get back to the Station accompanied by a bloodstained note reading *(Jack the Ripper voice)* Today her pancreas. Tomorrow all twenty six feet of her intenstines.

BARTHOLOMEW'S *forced laugh falls on stony ground.*

STENNING.
You won't be warned will you sir? I can see that.

He walks out slamming the front door.

Thoughtfully BARTHOLOMEW returns to the main room and pulls down the blind to cover the window, then his face breaks into a broad smile and he launches himself into a delighted caper of self-congratulation. Eventually he stops to examine himself in the mirror.

Mirror mirror on the wall
Who is the wiliest murderer of them all?
Unquestionably it is I — Norman Cresswell
Bartholomew, the Dorchester Dismemberer,
and noted Cop Kidder.

He preens himself, striking some more attitudes and making faces.

BARTHOLOMEW.
Well I suppose even self-congratulation must have a stop.
To our muttons.

He exits up the stairs, and after a short pause returns with the inert body of MILLIE. She is still naked. He lays her on the couch. A pause. He contemplates her, thoughtfully toying with a kitchen knife, as if about to start cutting her up. Suddenly she starts to stir. He drops the knife and gets her a glass of water, and sitting her up, forces her to drink it.

Here, drink this. You can't sleep your whole life away you know.

MILLIE

(drugged voice) What? . . . What happened?

She looks about herself and finds that she is naked.

Where are my clothes? . . . What am I doing here?

BARTHOLOMEW.
Surely you mean "Where am I?"

MILLIE.
(recovering full consciousness) What the hell's been going on.

BARTHOLOMEW.
Quite a lot actually. A whole rather touching charade in fact. I must say that your performance, though lacking somewhat in animation was most convincing.

MILLIE *rises and starts to dress.*

MILLIE.
What are you talking about? One moment I was sitting in that chair — the next I'm over here with all my clothes off.

BARTHOLOMEW.
Don't you remember. We were playing strip poker and you had rather a run of bad luck . . .

MILLIE.
Norman! Don't be tiresome.

31

BARTHOLOMEW.
What can I say? You passed out.

MILLIE.
What? Just like that?

BARTHOLOMEW.
Well with the help of a Mickey Finn I slipped you.

MILLIE.
What! You mean you drugged me?

BARTHOLOMEW.
Absolutely.

MILLIE.
Whatever for?

BARTHOLOMEW.
I needed your passive co-operation in a little game I was
playing.

MILLIE.
Really? What was it called — Hunt The Necrophiliac?

BARTHOLOMEW.
No. It was called Sergeant Stenning Meets the Cry-Wolf
Syndrome.

MILLIE.
Do you think we might take it from the top?

BARTHOLOMEW.
Surely. A drink?

MILLIE.
O.K.

BARTHOLOMEW.
Champagne?

MILLIE.
Fine.

BARTHOLOMEW *fetches the wine and starts to open it.*

BARTHOLOMEW.
Here we are, Veuve Cliquot.

MILLIE.
I wonder if they make a Veuf Cliquot.

BARTHOLOMEW.
H'm?

MILLIE.
Widower as opposite to widow. It's what you're aiming to become isn't it?

BARTHOLOMEW.
Oh I see. Yes, of course it is. I'm sorry darling, I haven't had the advantage of your Berlitz education. *(He fills the glasses and hands her one)* But I do know a little Latin. To uxoricide!

MILLIE.
It sounds like a venereal disease.

BARTHOLOMEW.
It means to wife-murder.

MILLIE *raises her glass gravely.*

MILLIE.
To wife-murder!

They drink.

MILLIE.
  I only hope the little game you've been playing has
  something to do with the subject.

BARTHOLOMEW.
  Oh, it had everything. You could say that I have been
  arranging the enabling factor, with you standing in for
  Elizabeth.

MILLIE.
  Will you explain, or do I have to play twenty questions?

BARTHOLOMEW.
  Patience, my sweet. Patience. You see, using your body
  I staged a strangulation, stripping and dismemberment in
  full view of Mrs. Ramage next door. She not unnaturally
  called Sergeant Stenning at the station, and he not
  unnaturally raced up here, only to find bits of a rather
  peachy little dummy I'd prepared bubbling away in the
  stove. I not unnaturally told him I was playing Buck
  Ruxton.

MILLIE.
  Good God, you didn't tell him about the games.

BARTHOLOMEW.
  It was necessary to mention a few. I told him I'd done
  Seddon, Chapman and Wainwright, and that I was thinking
  of doing Patrick Mahon.

MILLIE.
  Jesus. How did he take it?

BARTHOLOMEW.
  He wasn't a hundred per cent beatified by the experience,

but the point is it worked. Sergeant Stenning is now unquestionably in the crushing grip of the deadly Cry-Wolf syndrome.

MILLIE.
So you said before, but what the hell does that mean?

BARTHOLOMEW.
It means that now I could disembowel seventy three whirling dervishes in full sight of the neighbours and the police wouldn't interfere. *(MRS. RAMAGE'S voice)* Please officer come at once. That dreadful Mr. Bartholomew is at it again. He seems to be cutting up a spinning man dressed in a funny hat and white pyjamas? *(SERGEANT STENNING'S voice)* Oh we know all about that mum. It's quite in order. He's just re-creating the Mysterious Mevlevi Murders. *(Own voice)* No, I think I can safely say that in future any odd happenings around this house will be discounted. I could murder anyone here without attracting the least suspicion or interference. The police would just think it was one of my games.

MILLIE.
It all seems a rather elaborate way of going on to me.

BARTHOLOMEW.
Elaborate. Effective and above all enjoyable.

MILLIE.
Ah, now we come to it.

BARTHOLOMEW.
I may have pleasured myself a little in the doing, but why not?

MILLIE.
And me too possibly.

35

BARTHOLOMEW.
Tut! Tut! You were the merest object — a necessary prop.

MILLIE.
That's what I object to. Why did you have to knock me out?

BARTHOLOMEW.
Don't you see. You had to be inert. If I'd stuck a stiff dummy in the chair, Mrs. Ramage would never have believed it was a real body and she would never have called Sergeant Stenning.

MILLIE.
I could have acted it.

BARTHOLOMEW.
I didn't think you'd have wanted to.

MILLIE.
Why not? I've helped you before, haven't I? You've obviously forgotten that only last week I spent a whole afternoon in a half gale on Henley Common, dressed in stays and crinoline as Mary Blandy yelling "Gentlemen don't hang me high for the sake of decency". And the previous weekend you had me dressed in an ancient nursing costume pushing a two hundred and forty pound weight round the suburbs of Nottingham playing that hideous poisoner Dorothea Waddingham.

BARTHOLOMEW.
I assure you I haven't forgotten. Both were very affecting portrayals, my darling.

He goes to kiss her. She avoids it.

MILLIE.
Well then, that only makes it worse. To think you had this

game all worked out, and didn't say a single word to me about it. I don't think I like that very much Norman. After all I've done for you, it's decidedly mean spirited.

BARTHOLOMEW.
Millie, my angel you must realise that this was one game I didn't want you involved in.

MILLIE.
Exactly how much more involved can I get than being stripped and strangled in full view of the neighbours.

BARTHOLOMEW.
Oh much more. Mrs. Ramage didn't really see your face. In fact she thought you were Elizabeth. You see I took special care that under no circumstances in the future could you be labelled a willing accomplice.

MILLIE.
Gallante but unconvincing. I'd have adored to have heard that chat with Stenning.

BARTHOLOMEW.
I'm sorry. Actually I really needed to be alone to get the full flavour of Ruxton.

MILLIE.
Yes I rather suspected that was the truth. It doesn't matter. But you don't really believe that that crazy hoax will avert suspicion from this house do you?

BARTHOLOMEW.
Of course it will. I mean Stenning might be a bit sniffy. It's only natural. Promotion prospects dashed. No pictures in the paper, no dramatic appearance in the witness box, but on the whole he took it very well, and he certainly isn't going to come leaping up here the next time Mrs. Ramage reports the thud of axe on bone, or what have you. *(He*

puts his arm round her) Look I'll make it up to you, I
promise. There's a marvellous part for you in the Long
Compton Witchcraft Murders. You see the mistress of this
randy old farmer was found in a pig's trough with a
pentacle cut into each kneecap. It'll make a lovely day out
in the Cotswolds.

MILLIE.

(she draws away) You know what worries me most about
your tales, Norman is how poorly mistresses seem to come
off.

BARTHOLOMEW.

Don't you think you're being a trifle over sensitive?

MILLIE.

Not really. It's just that I'd like to hear about wives getting
it once in a while — particularly your wife. I've noticed
you've been a bit evasive about the whole subject.

BARTHOLOMEW.

Evasive?

MILLIE.

Non specific. Neglectful. Omissive.

BARTHOLOMEW.

Oh! You think that do you?

MILLIE.

I'm afraid I do, yes. For instance, when is she back?

BARTHOLOMEW.

Tomorrow night.

MILLIE.

And you'll do it then?

BARTHOLOMEW.

Absolutely. One more night of that road drill voice will
drive me into a strait jacket.

MILLIE.

I doubt whether it will drive you into being a murderer
however. And I really wonder whether you think it should.

BARTHOLOMEW.

Of course I do. We both know very well why I'm killing her.
She won't agree to divorce and we can't wait five years to
prove irretrievable breakdown unilaterally.

MILLIE.

I know all that, but I still don't believe you've actually
formed the intention to do it.

BARTHOLOMEW.

What on earth do you mean?

MILLIE.

Simply that *au fond* you're just a child who loves to play
mad, off-beat games. Admittedly you do them with great
thoroughness and panache, but they've got absolutely
nothing to do with solving the real problems in your life
whatever. I mean look at this murder. You've been playing
with the idea for ages, wondering whether you can actually
"cross the great divide between fantasy and reality" but
you're no nearer doing it now, then you were a month ago.
Old books and famous trials and playing at murderers are
one thing, but they're a pretty far cry from actually
bumping someone off yourself. I'm sorry Norman, but I've
got to say it. I don't think you're the stuff of which real
murderers are made.

BARTHOLOMEW.

For Christ's sake Millie shut up! I know I may have been a
bit dilatory, but these things need working out. I've already

taken the first step this evening. The second I will execute tomorrow night, and I can assure you it is a plan of mind-shattering cunning, and imagination.

MILLIE.
Oh, I'm sure it is . . . the broken neck induced by a dislodged stair rod, or piece of invisible twine tied to the banister; electrocution by impaired iron, or tampered toaster; poisoning by small doses of antimony administered over a long period as in the Charles Bravo case, disposal in a carboy of sulphuric acid as used by George Haig in his garage, and so on and so forth; but I'll bet my sainted Aunt Harriet's amber bangle that you've got nothing practical worked out, that won't have me visiting you in Parkhurst within the month.

BARTHOLOMEW.
God, you really are a bitch sometimes.

They glare at each other for a moment.

MILLIE.
Alright then, supposing you tell me what you have in mind.

BARTHOLOMEW.
(slowly still furious) Well, if you must know basically I am planning to use Christie's trick with the deck chair and gas pipe. It proved very effective with those half a dozen drabs he built into the wallpaper of ten Rillington Place.

MILLIE.
What was it?

BARTHOLOMEW.
It's really quite simple. I'll show you.

He dives down into the cellar and emerges with a deck chair which he proceeds to erect near the stove but facing

*away from it. He then takes up the gas poker which is lying
nearby attached to a long piece of rubber tubing and
unfastens it. The tubing he uncoils and leads over to the
deck chair.*

Now, if you'll just come here, and make yourself
comfortable.

MILLIE.
Wouldn't an armchair do as well? Do you have to use a deck
chair?

BARTHOLOMEW.
Well Christie did.

MILLIE.
Can you possibly see Elizabeth accepting a deck chair in the
middle of her living room without asking a few questions?

BARTHOLOMEW.
It's a good point. *(Reluctantly)* I suppose I could bring
myself to use the armchair.

*He collapses the deck chair and then faces the armchair
away from the stove and indicates that MILLIE should sit
in it. She does so. He gives her a bowl and covers her head
with a cloth. He then turns on the gas and tiptoes up behind
her holding the tube which now stretches halfway across the
room, and slowly advances it under her nose.*

BARTHOLOMEW.
Old Christie used to pretend he was a doctor, and could
cure women's ailments. Muriel Eady, his second victim, and
a life-time catarrh sufferer thought that she was inhaling
Friar's Balsam. Actually it was mixed with coal gas, and
when she became unconscious he had intercourse with her
while at the same time strangling her.

41

MILLIE, *who has been struggling during this speech to avoid the gas, now goes limp, unnoticed by the enthusiastic* BARTHOLOMEW.

Looking at the body afterwards he said "Once again I experienced that quiet peaceful thrill. I had no regrets."

He suddenly notices MILLIE's *condition.*

Here, are you alright?

He removes the cloth and turns the gas off. She returns to full consciousness, choking.

MILLIE.
Well I must say that's the nearest thing to a lethal act you've perpetrated all month.

BARTHOLOMEW.
Sorry. I didn't notice. I'll get you some water.

He pours a glass of water and brings it to her, drinking some himself before handing over the glass. She drinks greedily.

MILLIE.
I seem to be spending most of this evening unconscious.

BARTHOLOMEW.
Alright I've said I'm sorry.

MILLIE.
Look, I don't care how you kill your wife, as long as you don't kill me practising for it.

BARTHOLOMEW.
I got a bit carried away, that's all.

MILLIE.

Lucky I wasn't — in a coffin . . . It was a damn fool scheme in the first place. Elizabeth knows you're not a doctor . . . and she certainly wouldn't sit here calmly while you farted around with that ludicrous length of tubing.

BARTHOLOMEW.

I know all that. Can't you see I was only having a bit of fun.

MILLIE.

Fun?

BARTHOLOMEW.

Well getting even with you for sending me up. I'm sorry it went so far.

He kisses her.

MILLIE.

Alright.

BARTHOLOMEW.

I really do have an absolutely fool-proof scheme you know.

He starts to change into evening dress.

MILLIE.

Reading her your collected volumes of Famous British Trials, and boring her to death I suppose?

BARTHOLOMEW.

(sourly) Very droll.

MILLIE.

O.K. What is it?

BARTHOLOMEW.

I don't think I'll tell you now.

MILLIE.
Oh come on.

BARTHOLOMEW.
No. You're altogether too untrusting.

MILLIE.
Now don't play hard to get, Norman.

BARTHOLOMEW.
Sorry old bean. You'll just have to content your probing little soul in peace.

MILLIE.
Norman, I want to know.

BARTHOLOMEW.
Well, you'll have to wait and see I'm afraid. For one thing as I said I've no intention of making you an accessory before the fact.

MILLIE.
Oh pooh!

BARTHOLOMEW.
Sorry, my mind's made up. And now I must be off I'm afraid. It's the Dorchester Water Colour Society's annual cook-in tonight.

MILLIE.
I suppose you'll be back late and pissed?

BARTHOLOMEW.
I hope so.

MILLIE.
Well I don't think I'll wait around, for that.

BARTHOLOMEW.

How wise, darling. Besides I'm sure it would be just as well if you kept out of the way until after I'd done it.

MILLIE.

Why?

BARTHOLOMEW.

To paraphrase Lady Macbeth, She that's coming must be provided for, and I'd like to make all my preparations without distraction.

MILLIE.

You mean you still won't tell me your plan?

He kisses her.

BARTHOLOMEW.

I love you.

MILLIE.

Answer me.

BARTHOLOMEW.

Why is it that women don't realise that No *is* an answer?

He puts his overcoat on.

MILLIE.

Strange. In my experience it's men who don't.

BARTHOLOMEW.

I suppose both sexes have a recurring deafness. The Male through enobling passion. The Female through ineradicable curiosity. I'll phone you tomorrow. O.K.?

MILLIE.

Look, why don't you just admit you simply haven't got the

45

guts to do it?

BARTHOLOMEW.
(grimly) You'll see.

MILLIE.
Arrogant sod! You've no more got a plan for killing
Elizabeth than I have for becoming World Tree Felling
Champion.

BARTHOLOMEW.
(tight) Jolly witty. Goodnight.

MILLIE.
(half mocking, half seductive) Don't be cross Tiger. Look
why don't you try it on me. I'll play Elizabeth, and you can
show me how you're going to do it.

She pulls up her skirt and sits 1950's pin up style.

No? Too tarty for a Professional Woman? Well then, how
about this?

She changes her pose to a more demure one.

Demure but affectionate. Feminine yet responsible. Yes, I
think that's it . . . Now let me see . . . She would be reading
Diseases of the Scrotal Sack or some other learned medical
tome, while you cooked the evening meal. *(Imitating
ELIZABETH's voice)* "Din dins ready, darling," she says, or
rather "Is dinner ready Norman?" — that's more her isn't
it? Yes. "Is dinner ready Norman?" And suddenly you take
the carving knife or rather it being you, the 17th century
Chinese Executioner's sword, and creep up . . .

BARTHOLOMEW.
(tight) Goodnight Millie.

MILLIE.
  Have a lovely time darling with all your clever Bohemian
  Painter chumsies.

BARTHOLOMEW.
  Oh piss off.

MILLIE.
  (derisively) My hero.

  She storms out banging the door behind her.

BARTHOLOMEW.
  Well . . . I've got to do it now.

  He draws himself up and toasts himself in the mirror.

  Norman Cresswell Bartholomew — what a marvellous
  name for a Murderer! . . . but how?

SLOW BLACKOUT

Scene Two

The time is later the same evening.

The stage is in darkness, except for the bathroom which is lit. Through the semi-opaque glass of the door we can see the distorted shadow of ELIZABETH moving round inside. The taps are running and she walks from the wash basin to the bath carrying a bottle. She shakes the contents into the bath and stirs the contents around violently before turning off the taps. The radio is playing 'My Way'.

We hear a car arrive and then we hear the front door open and close. BARTHOLOMEW enters in evening dress. He is somewhat drunk. He crosses to centre stage, turns on a light and removes his overcoat. He mimes to the song 'My Way'.

BARTHOLOMEW.
    Yes, and I'll do it my way!

Suddenly he stops in his tracks as he sees his wife's fur coat and hat lying on a chair. Next to them is her suitcase. His gaze moves upwards to the bathroom where we can see the shadow of ELIZABETH putting on her bathcap. He scowls and turns on the radio.

BARTHOLOMEW.
    (to himself) Oh shit! . . . She's back a night early.

Angrily he throws his overcoat into a chair making a clatter. The louvred door opens a fraction to emit a great gust of steam. (Or alternatively if the gauzed bathroom is used, we can see a bath-capped figure moving about in it or getting into the bath).

ELIZABETH.
    (voice from bathroom) Hullo . . . Is that you Norman?

BARTHOLOMEW.
> *(forcing himself to speak pleasantly)* Oh hullo dear, I wasn't expecting you home till tomorrow.

ELIZABETH.
> *(voice from bathroom)* I had a change of plan. Bring me a brandy will you?

BARTHOLOMEW.
> O.K.

He crosses to the kitchen area and pours out the brandy. He is thinking furiously. He crosses the main room and stops at the foot of the stairs. Suddenly he is struck by a thought.

BARTHOLOMEW.
> *(to himself)* Of course! That's it! George Joseph Smith . . . The Brides in the Bath Murderer . . . Perfect! Bessie Munday at Herne Bay. Alice Burnham at Blackpool. Margaret Lofty at Highgate. He crept up behind them and slid their heads down under the water and held them there. Afterwards he played the harmonium. "Nearer My God To Thee" What could have been more tasteful?

He starts to strip.

ELIZABETH.
> *(voice from bathroom)* Norman! . . . Where's that drink?

BARTHOLOMEW.
> Coming.

He finishes undressing but retains his shorts. He tosses back the brandy and starts to ascend the stairs flexing his fingers.

SLOW CURTAIN

Act Two

Act II continues where Act I stopped.

NORMAN *stands outside the bathroom door, irresolute.*
With sudden resolve he cautiously opens the bathroom door
to its full extent. We see him approach the bath-capped
head almost overtopped by bubbles, and through the
swirling clouds of steam we watch the whole murder – the
head pushed under, the wildly threshing legs – the water
slopped over in the struggle, and then after an appreciable
time, the cessation of all movement.

BARTHOLOMEW *steps back and stares down at the inert*
mass of bubbles for a long moment. Satisfied that life is
extinct, he takes a towel, and leaves the bathroom, closing
the door behind him. There is a short satisfied pause. He
has actually done it, and is filled with great elation.

BARTHOLOMEW.
I've done it . . . I've actually done it! I felt the life force
slip away under my hands, I'm a murderer. I've joined the
'alien clan' and set my face against the world . . . *(He*
examines his face in a mirror) Norman Bartholomew, are you
you really one of those very special intrepid men who are
prepared to be damned? Have you in fact achieved the
most abandoned guilt which is the last and most irresistible
challenge to everlasting goodness? . . . I wonder. Perhaps
shame will come seeping in as the days pass to erode my
belief in the impossibility of forgiveness, and truly damn
me. I shall have to wait and see.

He wipes his glasses, then towels himself vigorously and
gathering up his clothes he retires to the bedroom whistling
cheerfully. After a few moments he returns wearing
sweater and slacks and moves downstairs where he sits
down at an antique harmonium and starts to sing and play,
the hymn 'Nearer My God to Thee'.

Not a dry fly in the house as they used to say at the

53

Windmill.

He rises from the harmonium and returns downstage.

BARTHOLOMEW.
(champagne mood) Now let's see. How to effect the
disappearing trick? The remote moorland grave? . . . The
weighted corpse in the canal? . . . the unclaimed trunk at
Victoria Station? . . . The packing case sent to foreign
parts? . . . The corpse in the blazing car? . . . The wrong
body in the churchyard? . . . Hell. I suppose the cellar's
still the safest.

*He takes a torch and exits stage left. We hear him open and
close the back door. After a few moments we again hear the
back door open and close, and he enters carrying a pick
axe, and spade. He moves over to the cellar door, opens it
and descends the steps.*
*Presently we hear the blows of the pick axe striking stone,
After a time this noise is replaced by the sound of the
spade shovelling earth. Both sounds are interspersed
through the ensuing monologue.*

(off. Parody Q.C's voice) Now Inspector Dew, perhaps you
would be kind enough to tell the members of the jury
exactly what it was you found in the cellar of number
thirty-nine Hilldrop Crescent . . . *(Inspector's voice)* We
found portions of a woman's body wrapped in a piece of
pyjama jacket. The head was missing, and to the best of my
knowledge still is. Identification however was effected
through known physical features, and items of personal
jewellery, and we are positive that the remains are those of
Kunigunda Makamotski, otherwise known as Belle
Elmore, otherwise known as Cora Crippen.

The front door bell rings.

(Q.C.'s voice) And have you been able to form any opinion

as the cause of death, Inspector? . . . *(Inspector's voice)* Yes
sir, we have. A post mortem revealed the presence of five
grains of hyoscine in the stomach. I have been informed
that that is far in excess of a fatal dose.

The front door bell rings again.

(Judge's voice) Hawley Harvey Crippen, it is now my
painful duty to pass sentence upon you, but before
proceeding to do so, I would ask you whether you have
anything to say in your own defence.

The front door opens, and SERGEANT STENNING *enters
a trifle hesitantly.*

STENNING.
    Hullo. Is anyone at home? Mr. Bartholomew?

BARTHOLOMEW
    (off from cellar. American-Crippen accent) I can only say
    that I know what I have done cannot be excused — only
    explained.

STENNING.
    Hullo. Mr. Bartholomew?

STENNING *closes the door and moves further into the
room to stand by the cellar door.*

BARTHOLOMEW.
    (off. American-Crippen voice) I killed my wife because of
    my very great love for the lady who honoured me by
    consenting to become my mistress. I expect no mercy, and
    deserve none. I am guilty and now have no recourse other
    than to accept my fate.

BARTHOLOMEW *emerges from the cellar, dishevelled and
dirty from work. He bypasses* STENNING *without seeing*

him, and heads for the drinks in the kitchen area.

STENNING.
>What are you guilty of Mr. Bartholomew?

BARTHOLOMEW *swings round, startled.*

BARTHOLOMEW.
>Christ! Where the hell did you spring from?

STENNING.
>I rang the bell a couple of times, sir, but was unable to attract your attention, so I took the liberty of stepping in.

BARTHOLOMEW.
>I see.

STENNING.
>You should keep your door locked you know.

BARTHOLOMEW.
>I forgot.

STENNING.
>I know it's the country, and you're supposed to trust people and all, but you'll only have yourself to blame if you get done.

BARTHOLOMEW.
>*(flustered)* Yes, you're quite right. I'm sorry.

BARTHOLOMEW *pours a shaky drink.*

STENNING.
>That's alright, sir. Now then what was it you were saying you were guilty of, just now?

BARTHOLOMEW *glances involuntarily at the bathroom,*

56

BARTHOLOMEW.
> Me? . . . Er . . . I'm not guilty of anything.

STENNING.
> I thought I heard you say you were, sir.

BARTHOLOMEW.
> No . . . not me.

STENNING.
> Well who were you talking to then?

BARTHOLOMEW.
> No one . . . I wasn't talking to anyone. I'm . . . I'm alone here.

STENNING.
> Very strange, sir. I could have sworn when I came in I heard voices. Perhaps in the circumstances I should take a quick look round.

He moves away as if to start a search but BARTHOLOMEW forestalls him.

BARTHOLOMEW.
> There's no need, Sergeant. What you heard was just another of my little charades. You see I'm digging a grave in the cellar — Crippen actually.

STENNING.
> Isn't he a bit obvious?

BARTHOLOMEW.
> Done to death you might say. Would you care to come down and have a look at it — view the "grisly remains".

STENNING.
>I've already warned you to stop playing these games, sir.
>You don't know what trouble you're inviting.

BARTHOLOMEW.
>Alright, Sergeant. Since it's an official request. *(He places his hand on his heart)* From now on I solemnly promise to give up murder. Though what I shall do in these long winter evenings without my innocent little hobby, I really don't know. Perhaps I'll take up serious drinking.

STENNING.
>*(looking at NORMAN's glass)* I thought you'd already started, sir.

BARTHOLOMEW.
>Only after I'd got in the house Sergeant, I assure you, so you can forget about your little bag of yellow crystals.

STENNING.
>Oh don't worry about that, sir. Though I did happen to notice, as I was passing just now that you'd left your car headlights on. I took the liberty of turning them off, by the way, you wouldn't want a flat battery in the morning.

He hands BARTHOLOMEW the keys.

BARTHOLOMEW.
>Thank you very much indeed. Most kind. I was wondering what you'd come about.

He pours himself a large whisky. STENNING observes this closely.

STENNING.
>*(meaningly)* I'm off duty now myself as a matter of fact. Just on my way home.

BARTHOLOMEW.
Oh, will you have a quick scotch?

STENNING.
Very kind of you, but beer's my drink.

BARTHOLOMEW.
Beer?

STENNING.
Yes. I think I see some there.

BARTHOLOMEW *looks at two quart bottles of beer standing among the drinks, and makes a feeble gesture towards them.*

Don't you trouble, sir. I'll manage. *(He takes the quart bottle and slowly empties it into a quart sized pewter tankard)*

BARTHOLOMEW *watches the operation with no great enthusiasm. Plainly his visitor is prepared to spend some time consuming his drink, and may need to use the facilities of the house, in course of time.*

BARTHOLOMEW.
I used to drink a lot of beer, once upon a time, but I gave it up. It was far too much exercise for the bladder.

STENNING.
I know what you mean. It's the same for me. In one end, and out the other — quick as a flash. But I can't afford shorts on a sergeant's pay, so I don't encourage myself to get the taste for them.

BARTHOLOMEW *shoots an uneasy glance in the direction of the bathroom.*

BARTHOLOMEW.
Cheers.

Both men raise their glasses. BARTHOLOMEW *takes a sip of his whisky.* STENNING *takes a huge draught of his, and than crosses unasked, to dump himself in a chair. Reluctantly* BARTHOLOMEW *moves to take a seat opposite him. There is a short silence during which* STENNING *swallows his beer contentedly.* BARTHOLOMEW *forces himself to talk equably.*

Well I'm sorry you've had to come here twice in one day to no real purpose.

STENNING.
It's all in the day's work.

BARTHOLOMEW.
I'll bet you were really a bit disappointed I wasn't actually a murderer — confess it.

STENNING.
I've already told you what I think about murder sir.

BARTHOLOMEW.
Well then, tell me about some of the murder cases you have been involved in, would I recognize them?

STENNING.
Some of them I expect.

BARTHOLOMEW.
Any real corkers?

STENNING.
Corkers?

BARTHOLOMEW.
Well like Peter Kurten, the Dusseldorf Monster for example.

60

He actually decapitated a swan and drank its blood, when he couldn't find any human beings to stab.

STENNING *looks coldly at* NORMAN *and shakes his head in reproof.*

STENNING.
Did you ever hear of Gerald Sandgate?

BARTHOLOMEW.
The Tattooed Galleon Murderer? Of course. Raped and killed four great grandmothers. Apparently he was just crazy for wizened flesh.

STENNING.
I was involved in that. Over nine million fingerprint comparisons were made. I got a commendation from the judge for being thorough. Not much in your line though I suppose. Not much to do with denying man's potential to see beauty.

STENNING *drinks up his beer. He examines the empty tankard suggestively, and looks around for a refill.*

BARTHOLOMEW.
(suggestively) Are you sure you won't have a quick scotch before you go?

STENNING.
No. If it's all the same to you, I'll stick to the beer.

He rises and starts to pour beer from another quart bottle. The sound of the beer pouring in the tankard irresistibly suggests urination, and BARTHOLOMEW *glances helplessly in the direction of the bathroom. He crosses and re-crosses his legs.* STENNING *sits.*

Another one you might have heard of was George Paling.

BARTHOLOMEW.
I don't recall him, I'm afraid.

STENNING.
R.A.F. Fitter. Ran his wife down in a car — an Austin A40
I think it was — no call me a liar, it was a Morris 1100.
Anyway he did it simply because she'd got on a bit and he'd
found himself a new fancy piece. To my way of thinking,
people like him are the worst. Just cunning and selfish —
killing their partners deliberately in cold blood. He was a bit
tricky at first, but I had a few minutes alone with him, and
I soon got to the heart of the matter. *(He drinks deeply)*

BARTHOLOMEW.
(Alarmed) What do you mean, Sergeant? What did you do?

STENNING.
I saw to it that he told the truth sir.

BARTHOLOMEW.
Yes. Yes. I see. Of course. One sometimes forgets that the
detective is almost as important as the murderer. It is his
work which helps the other to immortality. I mean, where
would the Yarmouth Beach Murderer be without the
pertinacity of Inspector Gough? . . . Or Raymond Morris
the Pixie Hood Murderer be, without the insights of
Superintendent Forbes? They complement each other don't
you see.

STENNING.
It's not like that sir, at all. But as I said before, you won't
be told.

He rises.

Anyway, that was very pleasant. I must be on my way.

BARTHOLOMEW.
Glad you enjoyed it. Goodnight.

STENNING.
> There's just one thing before I go. I wonder if I could use
> your toilet?

> NORMAN *stands thunderstruck as* STENNING *heads off up
> the stairs in the direction of the bathroom.* STENNING *is
> just about at the door when* BARTHOLOMEW *finds his
> voice.*

BARTHOLOMEW.
> Hey! Stop! Not in there.

STENNING.
> Sorry sir. This is the bathroom isn't it?

BARTHOLOMEW.
> Yes, yes of course. But . . . but the loo's blocked I'm afraid.
> Helplessly blocked. I've sent for a plumber, but you know
> how long they take to come round.

> STENNING *again turns to the door.*

STENNING.
> Oh I expect I can fix that. I'm a bit of a handyman myself.

> STENNING *opens the door so that the audience can see the
> legs of the drowned woman hanging over the side of the
> bath. He, still facing* BARTHOLOMEW, *cannot see them.*

BARTHOLOMEW.
> *(urgently)* Please Sergeant, I'd rather you didn't. It's all a bit
> messy.

> STENNING debates it for a moment then shrugs.

STENNING.
> Oh very well sir, if you insist. *(He closes the door and
> descends the stairs.)* I suppose you don't have another

toilet do you?

BARTHOLOMEW.
No I'm afraid we don't but you are very welcome to use the garden.

STENNING.
Then I suppose I better had.

BARTHOLOMEW *shows him out to the back garden, and then returns himself. He is in a high state of excitement and breathes deeply.*

BARTHOLOMEW.
(to himself) This is exactly how Christie must have felt when he discovered the skull of one of his earlier victims had accidentally become exposed in the garden where the police were searching for the body of Mrs. Evans. Extraordinary . . . The mind does work extremely swiftly under the circumstances.

STENNING *comes running in looking very embarrassed.*

That was a quick one Sergeant.

STENNING.
On the contrary, sir, just as I was about to . . . er . . . relieve myself, your neighbour Mrs. Ramage poked her head out of the window, so I had to desist. We'd never hear the end of it, if she was to catch the Law urinating.

BARTHOLOMEW.
That's for certain. Perhaps you'd care to use the Spode potty?

He offers an old chamber pot which has a flowerpot in it.

STENNING.
Everything's a big laugh to you sir, isn't it. But you'll see it

64

all quite differently one of these days, believe me.

He starts to leave the room, then stops.

By the way sir, heard from your wife?

BARTHOLOMEW.
Er no. As I told you, I think she's taken off.

STENNING.
You don't seem too upset at the prospect.

BARTHOLOMEW.
There's more to life than matrimony Sergeant. Goodnight.

STENNING.
Goodnight sir.

He gives BARTHOLOMEW *a long look from which the other flinches, then leaves.* BARTHOLOMEW *follows him into the hall. We hear the front door open and close.*

BARTHOLOMEW *re-enters the room and stands weakly against a wall breathing deeply. After a moment he collects himself and advances into the centre of the stage.*

BARTHOLOMEW.
Now then, where was I? . . . Ah yes. Stage two. The note.

He takes a sheet of notepaper and inserts it in the typewriter. He types rapidly for a minute, then pulls out the paper and reads it.

(reading) My darling Norman. I am going away with the man I love, and will never trouble you again. Please try to understand that when love commands, I have no choice but to obey, even if it means hurting the one man who has shown more gentleness, kindness, and understanding to me

than anyone else in the world. Farewell and try to forget me quickly. Your faithless Elizabeth.

He grins to himself delightedly, and places the note on the easel. He then goes out to the garden, and returns staggering under the weight of a large sack of quicklime, so marked.

At least I won't make the same mistake that Wainwright did with Chloride of Lime. I never did like well preserved women.

He carries the sack down into the cellar. We hear him spreading the lime in the cellar with a spade, whistling cheerfully as he works.

(slowly as if making it up)
There was an old doctor called Crippen
Whose ways were really quite rippin.
He took ticket of leave
With Ethel Le Neve
But fell foul of Canadian shippin.

Chuckling, BARTHOLOMEW *emerges from the cellar, brushing himself down, and plainly well satisfied with himself and his work.*

Good. Now for the interment.

He crosses the room and mounts the stairs to the bathroom. He opens the door and is about to go in when the doorbell rings. He stands frozen and indecisive. It rings again more imperiously. Quietly he closes the bathroom door, and tiptoes downstairs. It rings again as he exits to the hallway to answer it. We hear him open the door, and then after a substantial pause, he backs slowly into the room. His face wears an expression of cataclysmic shock. We hear the front door close, and then after a further pause a figure walks into the room, carrying a suitcase. It is his wife

ELIZABETH.

She is about forty, attractive, well turned out, about the same size as MILLIE. *She has about her an air of great competence and efficiency. She puts down her suitcase.*

BARTHOLOMEW.

My God . . . Elizabeth!

ELIZABETH.

Well come on, don't just stand there saying my God Elizabeth, as if you'd seen a ghost. Who the hell did you think it was? One of your silly old murderers come to pay a call? I forgot my key, that's all.

BARTHOLOMEW.

(dazedly) Elizabeth . . . ?

He looks helplessly upwards towards the bathroom.

ELIZABETH.

Exactly . . . Your dear wife Elizabeth. I didn't expect a rapturous welcome, but at least you might seem a bit more pleased to see me home.

BARTHOLOMEW *makes a great effort to pull himself together.*

BARTHOLOMEW.

But I don't understand. You're a day early. I didn't expect you till tomorrow.

ELIZABETH.

I know. But I had to postpone a Caesarian. Give me a hand with the cases will you.

She goes out through the front door. He looks round desperately and sees her fur coat and open suit case. He closes it and throws both into the cellar.

67

BARTHOLOMEW.

(looking up to the bathroom) So you did play Elizabeth
after all. Christ! . . . What have I done?

ELIZABETH.

(off) Come on. What's keeping you?

BARTHOLOMEW.

N . . . Nothing.

ELIZABETH.

(off) Then stop skyving, and give me a hand.

*He runs off. After a short pause they both return carrying
suitcases, which they put down in a corner of the room.*

God I'm tired. It really is a bloody long way. I think I'll
have a bath before I unpack.

BARTHOLOMEW.

(wildly) Why not have a drink first . . . Do you good.

ELIZABETH.

Alright. Give me a brandy.

ELIZABETH *takes off her coat and puts it away in the hall cupboard.* BARTHOLOMEW *looks agitatedly up the stairs, then
moves to make the drink. She returns and he hands it to her.*

ELIZABETH.

Didn't you have that Painter's dinner tonight?

BARTHOLOMEW.

Yes.

ELIZABETH.

I thought you had to dress for that.

BARTHOLOMEW.

I changed.

ELIZABETH.
What on earth for?

BARTHOLOMEW.
I wanted to be comfortable.

ELIZABETH.
Sloppy you mean. Like this room. All I have to do is to go away for a couple of days, and the whole place looks like a pig sty. You really expect me to clear up after you all the time, don't you?

BARTHOLOMEW.
I told you, I didn't expect you back tonight.

ELIZABETH.
I tried to phone you earlier, but there was no reply. Anyway, what's that got to do with the price of fish? Does it mean you have to live like a tramp while I'm away.

BARTHOLOMEW.
I live as I please.

ELIZABETH.
Like a tramp.

She starts to tidy up the room.

BARTHOLOMEW.
If you say so. Personally I think it's better than living like a Prussian Factory Inspector.

ELIZABETH.
Why don't you save your wit for that pneumatic little slut, whom I expect you've been seeing every day I've been gone.

BARTHOLOMEW.
Don't be ridiculous!

ELIZABETH.
Oh? Then has she finally become as bored with your nonsensical games as I did?

BARTHOLOMEW.
What?

ELIZABETH.
Yes. That's it, — or she'd be here now wouldn't she — since neither of you expected me home tonight? The only thing I can't understand is why it took her so long. I was catatonically disinterested in your homicide capers within a month. It's taken her three.

BARTHOLOMEW.
What utter piffle.

ELIZABETH.
You may find it peeving that your whore's sussed out she's been playing footsie with a ten year old child, but I suspect it certainly isn't piffle.

BARTHOLOMEW.
If you only knew how vulgar you looked when you spoke like that.

ELIZABETH.
When I speak the truth you mean.

BARTHOLOMEW.
It is not the truth. Millie was not . . . is not bored with me!

ELIZABETH.
She's bored alright. Rigidly, sempiternally, paraplegically bored.

BARTHOLOMEW.
No!

ELIZABETH.
    If she wasn't you'd be out with her now, scampering
    around tying her to trees, or rummaging through abattoirs,
    or throwing blood-stained parcels out of train windows, or
    wasting your time in some equally morbid manner. Why
    don't you think seriously about growing up, Norman?

BARTHOLOMEW.
    And why don't you think seriously about shutting up,
    Elizabeth?

    ELIZABETH *approaches very close to* BARTHOLOMEW.

ELIZABETH.
    If you want my opinion, giving you and your infantile
    fantasies the push, was the best day's work that sleazy little
    trollop of yours ever did.

BARTHOLOMEW.
    For Christ's sake, lay off Millie. At least she knows how to
    have fun. At least she doesn't spend all day with her nose
    buried in some dry old medical textbook. At least she
    knows which side is up!

ELIZABETH.
    Really? I'm surprised that as your girl friend, she ever learnt
    the meaning of the word up.

    They stare at each other.

BARTHOLOMEW.
    Thanks a lot. What a charitable lady you are to be sure.

ELIZABETH.
    I'm sorry. I'm tired. I'd better have that bath now.

BARTHOLOMEW.
    Have another drink.

ELIZABETH.
>Alright. Just one.

He pours a drink and hands it to her.

Why don't you try with me any more?

BARTHOLOMEW.
>I do. I do try. But mostly nothing comes. It's as if I'd never known anything in my entire life — not a single physical fact — not a story — not the tiniest scrap of memorabilia. Nothing . . . *(He laughs)* They do say the memory goes first.

ELIZABETH.
>Not so. It's the urge to search it that goes first. The trouble is that in the last twelve years I've made you feel so secure, you've gone quite numb. I have the effect on you of six seconal and a comfort blanket. It's my fault I suppose.

She reaches to touch his hand. He endures it.

BARTHOLOMEW.
>No.

ELIZABETH.
>Yes. It must always be the fault of the ones who suffer — they're such rancidly bloody fools.

BARTHOLOMEW.
>No more foolish than people trying to protect a pretty ropey investment.

ELIZABETH.
>By throwing good money after bad you mean?

They smile at each other.

Like that time in the South of France when you had to pay

for that perfectly foul meal, and then fell off the patio and rolled down the hill . . .

BARTHOLOMEW.
I know. Into all those hideous thorn bushes.

ELIZABETH.
And the goats . . . Remember the goats?

BARTHOLOMEW.
Do I ever! Between them they cut my silk suit to ribbons. First time on, too.

ELIZABETH.
And you hadn't even paid for it . . .

BARTHOLOMEW.
It was eighty quid — even in those days.

They laugh companionably. Then the laughter subsides.

ELIZABETH.
What was the name of that village — Ouly Ourly . . .

BARTHOLOMEW.
Ouchy sur Fleuve. You know that reminds me of the most extraordinary thing I found out later.

ELIZABETH.
Oh what was that?

BARTHOLOMEW.
James Berry, the official English executioner between 1884 and 1892, actually lived there for a while.

ELIZABETH.
(stiffening) Really.

73

BARTHOLOMEW.
Yes. Only the other day I was reading his account of the execution of a Mrs. Jane Cassidy, a woman who murdered her lover during a drunken quarrel. *(Declamatory)* She walked to the scaffold with a free firm stride, defying the world which had so justly punished her. But when the rope touched her neck, she blushed crimson to the very roots of her hair, and her lips twitched convulsively. Intense shame and sorrow were never more plainly expressed by any woman. *(Normal voice)* Fantastic eh?

ELIZABETH.
Fantastic! Why don't you try and woo Millie back by asking her to play the part of that woman. I'm sure she'd be only too happy to do it, except of course she's probably not had too much experience of expressing intense shame.

BARTHOLOMEW.
Very funny.

ELIZABETH.
I really am going to have that bath now. I'm operating at 9 a.m. and believe it or not, bringing a little life into the world takes even more effort and concentration than bringing a little death.

Under BARTHOLOMEW's *appalled gaze she starts up the stairs towards the bathroom.*

BARTHOLOMEW.
(desperate) Aren't you going to put the car away first?

ELIZABETH.
No. I can't be bothered. It can stay out tonight like yours.

BARTHOLOMEW.
Mine starts alright. You know you always have trouble.

ELIZABETH.

    Look, I'm bloody tired. I've just driven all the way down from Birmingham. If you were any kind of man at all you'd put the flaming car in the garage yourself. *(She takes another couple of steps up the stairs)*

BARTHOLOMEW.

    (mimicking her) It's your car. But of course if you want me to clear up after you all the time . . .

ELIZABETH.

    Alright, I'll put the sodding thing away myself. *(She storms down the stairs, across the room and out of the front door.*

    BARTHOLOMEW *runs up the stairs and into the bathroom. We see him scoop the dead body out of the bath, and carry it, wet and still flecked with soap bubbles to the head of the stairs, and start down them. The head falls back, and we see clearly that it is the body of* MILLIE. *We hear the car door slam furiously outside and footsteps approaching. The front door slams as* BARTHOLOMEW *retreats hurriedly up the stairs and back into the bathroom, closing the door.* ELIZABETH *enters.*

ELIZABETH.

    The damned keys are in my coat. I can't be bothered with it any more . . .

    She sees that BARTHOLOMEW *isn't there and stumps closely into the bedroom.*

    Norman, where are you?

    BARTHOLOMEW *slips out of the bathroom and down the stairs, bumping into* ELIZABETH *who comes out of the bedroom.*

    What the hell are you doing, capering about all over the

place. Out of my way.

She pushes him aside and walks up the stairs towards the bathroom. He slowly retreats stage centre looking up, petrified. She goes into the bathroom and closes the door. There is a slight pause, then a sudden sharp scream. The door of the bathroom is then thrown open and ELIZABETH staggers out and totters down the stairs to face BARTHOLOMEW. The bathroom door swings shut behind her. Alternatively of course, if gauze is used we will actually see ELIZABETH discover the body. There is a long silence between them.

BARTHOLOMEW *nods his head vigorously.*

BARTHOLOMEW.
 . . . It was an accident.

ELIZABETH.
 An accident?

BARTHOLOMEW.
 Yes.

ELIZABETH.
 You mean she slipped and struck her head — something like that?

BARTHOLOMEW.
 (rallying) Yes. That's what happened.

ELIZABETH.
 How do you know?

BARTHOLOMEW
 I mean that's what must have happened.

ELIZABETH.
 You weren't in the bathroom at the time though?

76

BARTHOLOMEW.
No.

ELIZABETH.
But you heard a crash. A cry?

BARTHOLOMEW.
Yes.

ELIZABETH.
Which?

BARTHOLOMEW.
Er . . . both. I ran up, but I couldn't see her for the bubbles.

ELIZABETH.
Bubbles?

BARTHOLOMEW.
She had a bubble bath. A huge one. I expect most of them
have subsided by now.

ELIZABETH.
Yes.

BARTHOLOMEW.
And the steam of course. That also made it very difficult to
see. There was a lot of steam.

ELIZABETH.
And?

BARTHOLOMEW.
Her head had gone under the water. Her legs were in the air.
I tried to get her out, but the bubbles made it too slippery.
I felt her pulse, and tried a mirror on her breath, but she
was unquestionably dead, so I left her there.

ELIZABETH.
How long ago was this?

BARTHOLOMEW.
Half an hour.

ELIZABETH.
Have you called the police?

BARTHOLOMEW.
No.

ELIZABETH.
Why not?

BARTHOLOMEW.
I don't know.

ELIZABETH.
What do you mean . . . You don't know?

BARTHOLOMEW.
I don't know.

ELIZABETH.
Why haven't you called the police?

BARTHOLOMEW.
(shouting) I don't know!

ELIZABETH.
Really? I think I do. It wasn't an accident was it?

BARTHOLOMEW.
Yes. Of course it was.

ELIZABETH.
Not the way I see it! You killed her.

BARTHOLOMEW.
    I . . .

ELIZABETH.
    What was it? Some wretched little sex romp that went wrong?

BARTHOLOMEW.
    No . . . no . . . of course not.

ELIZABETH.
    (with dawning understanding) Or was it one of your stupid
    murderer games?

BARTHOLOMEW.
    No.

ELIZABETH.
    Yes. That's more like it isn't it. What were you playing
    Brides in the Bath?

BARTHOLOMEW.
    I told you it was an accident. I didn't mean . . .

ELIZABETH.
    No, I don't suppose you did. But that's what happens if
    you don't grow up. You kill people, but you don't mean to.
    (Relentless) In my book that's worse almost than killing
    people and actually meaning to. At least one is the act of a
    man who has taken a conscious decision, while the other is
    just the work of a lunatic child. They'll find out she was
    your mistress, of course.

BARTHOLOMEW.
    How? None of her friends knew about me.

ELIZABETH.
    Your wife away. A naked girl in your bathroom at night.
    Do you think they'd believe she was the plumber's mate

come to fix the U bend?

BARTHOLOMEW.
It could still be an accident. What's my motive? I wanted her alive.

ELIZABETH.
Many men have killed importuning mistresses with whom they have become bored. Surely I don't have to remind the famous murder expert of that?

BARTHOLOMEW.
I suppose you're right.

ELIZABETH.
You're not doing very well, really, are you?

BARTHOLOMEW.
Sorry. I'm a bit numb — not thinking.

ELIZABETH.
So I see. Don't you think it's about time you started?

BARTHOLOMEW.
Yes.

ELIZABETH.
Well suppose you begin by telling me what actually did happen.

BARTHOLOMEW.
You were right. I was playing George Joseph Smith — The Brides in the Bath Murderer, and I must have gone too far. One minute we were laughing and joking, and the next — well she was just lying there under the water — dead.

ELIZABETH.
Well it's Life if they believe that you meant to kill her, and

at least five years if they believe you didn't.

BARTHOLOMEW.
And nothing if they believe it was an accident.

ELIZABETH.
I don't think it's very likely they'll do that.

BARTHOLOMEW.
They will if you support me. I mean you're a doctor.
Couldn't you say that it's happened since you've been back.
That you returned home unexpectedly . . . that I confessed
to you that Millie was upstairs taking a bath, and that
suddenly we heard a cry, but by the time we'd got the door
broken down it was too late.

ELIZABETH *looks at him thoughtfully for a long moment.*

ELIZABETH.
I need a drink.

BARTHOLOMEW, *a half smile on his face moves to pour
her a glass of brandy. She follows him, and he gives her the
drink which she sips thoughtfully.*

BARTHOLOMEW.
Well, what do you say?

ELIZABETH.
Would you mind telling me just why I should stick my neck
out for you?

BARTHOLOMEW.
To protect your name for one thing. I'm sure future
patients won't rush to be treated by a woman doctor whose
husband killed his mistress in the course of what they will
all take to have been "a wretched little sex romp". You'll
have to leave the neighbourhood, you know — give up your

practice, change your name, and go and live in self-enforced
obscurity. I can see you now, crouched over the cruet set in
the dining room of an Eastbourne boarding house, timidly
forking up the tomato sauce covered rissoles as you wait for
the inevitable glance of recognition that will send you on
your weary way again.

ELIZABETH.

Oh phooey! You don't really think the world's like that
any more do you. Much though it may offend against your
ridiculous theories, it's got far too violent for people to care
all that much about one little murder. It'll probably be
tough for a few weeks, but they'll soon forget.

BARTHOLOMEW.

Not as quickly as all that . . . You may be very sure that if I
find myself in the dock through your failure to help me, my
spicy embellishments will make it not only the murder trial
of the century, but also one in which you figure unforget-
tably. *(Supplicant's voice)* Ladies and gentlemen of the
jury, I must confess that it was my wife who first
introduced me to strange and recondite forms of love
making, in which bubble baths, rubber wear, and even live
dog fish all figured prominently.

ELIZABETH.

Can't you shut up fantasising for a moment. It's not enough
I suppose that your stupid games have actually led you to
kill someone, without your wanking away about what
you're going to do at the trial.

BARTHOLOMEW.

(hard) I'm merely showing you how absolutely intolerable I
could make life for you if I chose.

*They regard each other with mutual loathing. She,
recognising the truth of what he is saying, flinches away,
and starts to walk abstractedly about the room.*

82

ELIZABETH.
(bitterly) You'd better let me think.

After several moments she moves to stand very close to him, looking into his face.

May I ask what you were planning to do with the body before I got here?

BARTHOLOMEW.
The cellar. Quicklime. Pretty old hat I'm afraid, but serviceable.

ELIZABETH.
Serviceable my arse. A single anxious phone call from one of her relatives, and the police would have it up before it had dried. If I go along with it at all, it will have to be the accident.

BARTHOLOMEW.
Yes. Alright.

ELIZABETH.
And furthermore I shall not expect to hear any further talk of divorce or separation or whatever, and of course there'll be no more mistresses.

BARTHOLOMEW.
So that's your price?

ELIZABETH.
Yes, and a pretty modest one I'd have thought for making oneself an accessory after the fact of manslaughter. Well, do you agree?

BARTHOLOMEW.
A lifetime's representation to the outside world of hard core connubial bliss?

ELIZABETH.
Exactly. Together we will uphold the sanctity of the
marriage contract.

BARTHOLOMEW *thinks gloomily about the proposition.*

BARTHOLOMEW.
(heavily) Alright.

ELIZABETH.
Well you'd better start filling in the cellar. I don't want
anything suspicious here when the police come.

ELIZABETH *goes to the cellar door, opens it and peers
down into it.*

My, you have been a busy little bee here haven't you. That's
quite a corking little grave you've dug.

*Her attention is caught by the sight of her case and coat.
She ducks down and returns with them.*

What on earth are these doing in the cellar! *(She holds up
the suitcase and coat, for* BARTHOLOMEW *to see)*

BARTHOLOMEW.
(uneasily) I don't know. You must have put them there.

ELIZABETH.
Me? Whatever for?

BARTHOLOMEW.
How would I know? *(He starts up the stairs to the
bathroom)*

ELIZABETH.
Just a minute. There's something very funny going on here.
What the devil are my fur coat and suitcase doing in the

cellar?

BARTHOLOMEW.
Search me.

ELIZABETH.
Well, either you put them there, or that girl put them there.
Which?

BARTHOLOMEW.
(shrill) I keep telling you, I don't know.

ELIZABETH *paces up and down, thinking deeply.*

ELIZABETH.
It's funny. When I came in tonight, your surprise at seeing
me was quite out of proportion to my merely arriving a
night early. It wasn't simply distress at having a dead body
on your hands. It was surprise . . . No — it was amazement!
Now why I ask myself, should you be *amazed* to see me?

BARTHOLOMEW *is quite unable to move. He makes a
helpless gesture.*

ELIZABETH.
Obviously you didn't expect to see me again, either then
or ever.

BARTHOLOMEW *gives an involuntary cry.*

You know what I'm saying, don't you Norman. I'm saying
that it wasn't your mistress you meant to kill. It was me!

BARTHOLOMEW.
No!

ELIZABETH.
How did the mistake happen . . . something I suppose to do

with the steam . . . the bubble bath . . . the head turned
away from you as you entered, wearing my bath cap . . .
the body shrouded in bubbles and steam . . . the face
invisible under the foamy water . . . My God!!

BARTHOLOMEW *tries to take hold of her, but she shakes
him off fiercely.*

BARTHOLOMEW.
Don't be ridiculous Elizabeth. I know the difference
between you and her.

ELIZABETH.
Obviously you didn't. I was the person you wanted out of
the way, not her.

BARTHOLOMEW.
No!

ELIZABETH.
Yes. Now let me think exactly how it all came about. You
had a dinner date this evening, so you couldn't have had one
with Millie. Nor did either of you expect me home tonight.
Did she try and play a joke on you — is that it? . . . Did she
creep in here and put this case and coat down to make you
think as you came in that I had returned? . . . Of course!
That's it! It *was* a game she was playing. Oh my God, the
old bitch has come back a day early. Surprise, surprise it's
your yummy little sex kitten after all, contentedly purring
away in the bath tub. But it went wrong, didn't it? You
returned, a bit boozed, thought she was me, shot upstairs
and shoved her head under the water before she had a
chance to show who she was. Jesus Christ!

BARTHOLOMEW.
You can't really believe anything as stupid as that.

ELIZABETH.
Or was it worse than that? Was she your accomplice in the

86

plan to murder me . . . And had she realised what a feeble partner she'd got, all talk and no do. I wonder — was it that she wanted to try you out — to see whether if she could persuade you that she was me, all helpless in the bath, you actually had the guts to try and do the murder.

BARTHOLOMEW.
(realising this might be the truth) No! She wouldn't have done that.

ELIZABETH.
It doesn't really matter. Either way she got her come-uppance, the poor cow.

BARTHOLOMEW.
(desperate) I swear to you on my life it wasn't like that. If you want to know, *I* borrowed the case and coat. It was part of my Brides in the Bath charade. Don't you see we were meant to be honeymooners newly arrived at our lodgings. When you went out to the van before, I pushed them into the cellar as obviously I didn't want you to see them.

ELIZABETH.
Is that the truth?

BARTHOLOMEW.
Yes. Absolutely.

ELIZABETH.
Then why didn't you tell me about it before?

BARTHOLOMEW.
I don't know . . . I was flustered . . . Somehow, I suppose I didn't want to make myself look more of a fool than I already was. Help me now, and I promise I'll stay with you and there'll be no more girl friends or talk of divorce.

She stares at him thoughtfully, evaluating the situation. He

87

moves towards her, and holds her by the shoulders looking sincerely into her eyes.

Look, if you honestly do believe that I am a murderer, and that it was you I tried to murder there is no point in our trying to go on together is there. You must phone Sergeant Stenning now, and turn me in.

ELIZABETH.
(slowly) Alright, Norman. I'll give you the benefit of the doubt. Perhaps there is something we can still make out of this life together — after all we had it once.

BARTHOLOMEW.
Yes, we did, it's true. I promise I'll try.

They kiss tenderly. BARTHOLOMEW is the first to break.

BARTHOLOMEW.
Perhaps we should call the police soon. They'll be able to tell won't they if we delay too long?

ELIZABETH.
From the rigor you mean? . . . Yes I suppose so. Will you do it or will I?

BARTHOLOMEW.
Perhaps it would come better from you — being a doctor. I'll go up and make poor Millie look a bit decent, and then I'll fix the cellar.

ELIZABETH.
What strange bargains we strike in our life!

BARTHOLOMEW.
Yes. But I swear you won't regret this one.

They exchange a fond look, then he moves to take a

*travelling rug from the back of a sofa, and walks up the
stairs to the bathroom. His expression changes to one
of smug self-satisfaction.* ELIZABETH *moves to the phone,
and having selected the police station number from a list on
the desk, she dials it. While waiting for an answer she
suddenly notices* BARTHOLOMEW's *"Leaving" note
pinned to the easel. She puts the phone down, and moves
nearer to read it.*

ELIZABETH.
(reading) My darling Norman. I am going away with the
man I love and will never trouble you again . . . *(She
continues to read silently)* Farewell, and try to forget me
quickly. Your faithless Elizabeth.

BARTHOLOMEW *freezes in horror. Like an automaton he
turns to face her. There is a long silence between them.*
ELIZABETH *does not immediately turn round to face him.*

So I was right. You bloody bastard!

*She starts shaking violently, and suddenly turns round to
show us that she is laughing uncontrollably.*

Well, well, well. If this isn't the best thing ever. The great
murder expert plots and plans his first actual crime with
fiendish cunning, and can't even get the victim right. *(She
breaks up laughing hysterically)*

BARTHOLOMEW.
(hissing) Shut up!

ELIZABETH.
Oh my dear, it's far too late to tell me to shut up. Every-
one's going to hear about this. You'll get your precious
notoriety alright — as a laughing stock. They'll probably
have a wax effigy of you in The Chamber of Horrors at
Madame Tussauds — Norman Bartholomew The Bubble

Bath Murderer. Drowned his lover in mistake for his wife.

She resumes laughing. He, now totally out of control, runs down the stairs and flies at her. Grasping her round the throat he starts to throttle her.

BARTHOLOMEW.
Shut up! Shut up! Shut up!

Suddenly she goes limp and faints to the floor. Dazedly he stands looking down at her, then stoops to check her state of health.

(to himself) H'm, only fainted. *(He picks her up and puts her on the sofa)* Oh God, this is a disaster . . . There must be something I can do . . . but what? . . . Now steady . . . Think!

He stands looking down at her, thinking. Gradually light dawns. He turns away and paces.

(slowly, thinking it through) Yes, that's it . . . She had a motive, for getting rid of my mistress . . . but I didn't . . . So what happend? . . . Let's see now. I'm out taking a walk to clear my head after the alcoholic excess of my dinner . . . While I'm out she comes home unexpectedly — finds Millie making herself at home in *her* bath — she's absolutely livid — a sudden temptation she pushes her under and holds her there . . . And then remorse and suicide . . . Yes, that's perfect.

He crosses to the sofa, and stoops to examine her throat with great attention.

Good. No bruises on the neck. Thank God she fainted when she did.

He drags her to the stove and lays her down beside it. Then

*he fetches a cushion from the divan, opens the oven door,
and arranges her comfortably with her head in the oven.*

BARTHOLOMEW.
Now then, is there anything I've missed?

*He looks around the room, and suddenly sees the note on
the easel.*

Ha! Glad I spotted you. You could have been the "one
mistake all murderers make". *(He burns it in the stove)*
Good! . . . Anything else? Of course! Her dress. The sleeves
and front would be wet. Good thinking N.B. You really are
behaving like a classic Murderer now.

*He gets a bowl of water from the sink and throws it over
her dress. Then he turns on the gas. We hear it hissing loudly
for a while. BARTHOLOMEW watches delightedly.
Suddenly the gas stops.*

Damn. The bloody cylinder's empty.

*He runs over to the kitchen area and starts quickly
changing over to a full gas cylinder.*

Sodding thing . . . I don't know why we can't be on the
mains like everybody else.

*At last his job is successfully completed and we hear the
hiss of gas start again. Behind his back, ELIZABETH has
revived and has taken the spit out of the oven. He crosses
to the cooker to check that all is well. He kneels down
feeling for her pulse. With a sudden savage movement she
sits up and stabs him in the stomach with the spit. He reels
back screaming, leaving the spit in ELIZABETH's hands.
Blood pours out through his fingers as he seeks to keep the
wound closed. ELIZABETH rises from the floor, turns off
the gas, and runs retching into the kitchen for a glass of*

91

water. Recovered, she returns to him.

BARTHOLOMEW.
My God . . . My God you bitch, what have you done?

BARTHOLOMEW runs to the window. He pulls aside the curtain and opens it.

Mrs. Ramage . . . Mrs. Ramage, help me. I've been stabbed.

He holds out his bloody hands.

Help . . . Help! . . . Call an ambulance.

A long pause. Then he registers hopelessness caused by her rejection, and topples back into the room.

Bloody cow!

ELIZABETH pulls the curtains closed.

ELIZABETH.
Wouldn't she listen to you Norman? Well it's hardly surprising is it? A man wholly obsessed with negative forces like murder and murderers must eventually forfeit all protection, and put himself in the way of harm.

BARTHOLOMEW.
Help me!

ELIZABETH opens her suitcase, and takes out a case containing surgeon's scalpels. Very deliberately she selects one.

BARTHOLOMEW.
What are you doing?

Slowly she approaches him.

ELIZABETH.
>I'm doing you a favour, Norman. I'm showing you what the murder game is really all about.

>*She slashes him four times with the scalpel across the chest and arms. He screams and tries to protect himself as blood spurts out through the torn shirt.*

>Well, darling, tell me — does it represent a mirror image of man's potential to realise bliss?

>*She slashes him again. He screams again.*

ELIZABETH.
>Is it truly our most daring challenge to God?

>*Another slash. Another scream.*

>Is this really a way to salvation? Is it Norman? . . . Is it? . . . Is it? . . . Is it?

>*She cuts away at him in a frenzy. Finally he collapses on the floor, and she moves away in a daze to sit on the stairs. There is a long silence.*

ELIZABETH.
>*(emotionally drained)* Norman . . . Norman . . . listen to me . . . It's worth listening to, because you see you've finally made a convert. *(Hysterical laugh)* Do you know what story I'll tell the police when they get here. I'll say I came in and found your mistress in my bath. In a sudden, uncontrollable burst of passion I drowned her and then killed you. It will be *my* murder.

>*In his terrible pain,* BARTHOLOMEW *somehow realises the significance of what she is saying.*

BARTHOLOMEW.
>*(very weak)* What!! . . . You can't do that. I killed. It was

93

my murder.

ELIZABETH *smiles a wicked smile at him, and slowly shakes her head as she takes away from him all he has left.*

ELIZABETH.
No, I think not. Did you really think that an inept little man like you could challenge the great moral laws of this universe. Mediocrity, my darling, has no theological status.

BARTHOLOMEW.
I had my vision.

ELIZABETH.
Vision! The eye of the heroic murderer does not fall on the wrong person.

She stirs him with her foot, then slowly, as she speaks, moves to sit on the stairs, still holding the scalpel.

ELIZABETH.
You know this really could be the crime passionelle of the century. I can see myself in the witness box now, proud, aloof, mysterious. All eyes will be upon me as I weave my bloody tale of wronged womanhood, omitting no ghastly detail of the drowning of my rival, and the slaughter of my husband. Believe me, my own dearest Norman, I will have, what you have always wanted — a true and abiding notoriety.

BARTHOLOMEW.
(a great cry) No. It's mine!! . . .

He collapses. There is a sudden loud knocking on the front door.

STENNING.
Open up. Police!

ELIZABETH *looks vaguely in the direction of the door,
but being virtually in a state of catatonia, is unable to move.
There is further knocking, then STENNING comes crashing
into the room through the back door. He sees
BARTHOLOMEW huddled on the floor, but does not at
first notice Elizabeth.*

Still playing games eh, Mr. Bartholomew? Well . . . this time
you've gone too far. You frightened Mrs. Ramage half to
death showing yourself to her all covered in blood. She just
called me in a fair old state, I can tell you. You may know
the difference between Kensington Gore, as you call it, and
the real stuff. Old ladies don't. I warned you twice today,
and that's enough. Do you hear me? Good God man, look
at me when I'm talking to you. I'm arresting you for a
breach of the peace.

BARTHOLOMEW *doesn't move.*

Oh come on!

STENNING *grabs BARTHOLOMEW and lifts him into a
sitting position. Then he sees his hideous mutilations.*

Christ Almighty!

*He kneels to examine him, then straightens up.
BARTHOLOMEW's lifeless body slips from his arms.
ELIZABETH drops the scalpel with a clatter. STENNING
turns to look at her. There is a pause.*

STENNING.
(slowly) I told him to stop in time. I told him he didn't
know the game he was playing. I told him it was the victim
who looked for the murderer.

ELIZABETH.
You were right, Sergeant. But he didn't have to look very

far. We made the appointment — years ago.

She leans against the banisters sobbing, and laughing as the

CURTAIN FALLS